TAPESTRY OF FAITHS:
THE TORAH, BIBLE, AND QURAN

ONESIMUS MALATJI

Copyright © 2023 ONESIMUS MALATJI
All rights reserved.

Tapestry of Faiths: The Torah, Bible, and Quran
By: Onesimus Malatji

Copyright ©2023 by Onesimus Malatji
Cover Design by CiX Connect
Interior Design by CiX Connect

Trademark Notice:

All trademarks mentioned within this book belong to their respective owners.

All rights reserved. No part of this publication may be reproduced, distributed, or transmitted in any form or by any means, including photocopying, recording, or other electronic or mechanical methods, without the prior written permission of the publisher, except in the case of brief quotations embodied in critical reviews and certain other non-commercial uses permitted by copyright law.

For permissions requests, contact the publisher at:
ony@cixconnect.co.za

Copyright Violation Warning:
Unauthorized reproduction or distribution of copyrighted material is against the law. Any unauthorized copying, distribution, or use of material from this book may result in legal action.
Fair Use Notice: This book may contain copyrighted material used for educational and illustrative purposes. Such material is used under the "fair use" provisions of copyright law.

Disclaimer:
The information provided in this book is for general informational purposes only. The author and publisher are not offering legal, financial, or professional advice. Readers are advised to consult appropriate professionals for advice specific to their individual situations.
Accuracy Disclaimer: While every effort has been made to ensure the accuracy of the information presented in this book, the author and publisher cannot be held responsible for any errors, omissions, or inaccuracies.

Fair Use Notice: This book may contain copyrighted material used for educational and illustrative purposes. Such material is used under the "fair use" provisions of copyright law.

Third-Party Content:

This book may reference or include content from third-party sources. The author and publisher do not endorse or take responsibility for the accuracy or content of such third-party material.

Endorsements:

Any endorsement, testimonial, or representation contained in this book reflects the author's personal views and opinions. It does not imply an endorsement by any third party.
Results Disclaimer: The success stories and examples mentioned in this book are not guarantees of individual success. Actual results may vary based on various factors, including effort and circumstances.

Results Disclaimer:

The success stories and examples mentioned in this book are not guarantees of individual success. Actual results may vary based on various factors, including effort and circumstances.
No Guarantee of Outcome: The strategies, techniques, and advice provided in this book are based on the author's experiences and research. However, there is no guarantee that following these strategies will lead to a specific outcome or result.

Fair Use Notice:

This book may contain copyrighted material used for educational and illustrative purposes. Such material is used under the "fair use" provisions of copyright law.

ACKNOWLEDGMENTS

I extend my deepest gratitude to everyone who has been a part of this incredible journey, both seen and unseen. Your support, encouragement, and unwavering belief in me have been the driving force behind the creation of this book.

To my family, for standing by me through thick and thin, for believing in my dreams, and for being a constant source of inspiration – your love and encouragement have been my guiding light.

To my friends, mentors, and colleagues, your valuable insights and feedback have shaped the ideas within these pages. Your willingness to share your wisdom and experiences has enriched this work beyond measure.

To all those who have supported me on my path, whether through a kind word, a helping hand, or a moment of shared understanding, thank you. Your presence in my life has made all the difference.

To the countless individuals who have faced challenges and setbacks, yet continued to strive for greatness, your stories have fuelled the inspiration behind these words. May you find solace and encouragement within these pages.

And finally, to the readers who have embarked on this journey with me, thank you for allowing me to share my thoughts and experiences. It is my hope that this book serves as a beacon of hope, a source of guidance, and a reminder that fulfilment can be found in every step of life's intricate tapestry.

With heartfelt appreciation,

Onesimus Malatji

TAPESTRY OF FAITHS:
THE TORAH, BIBLE, AND QURAN

TABLE OF CONTECT   PAGES

Introduction	8-10
Overview of the Project	11-13
Importance Of Interfaith Understanding	14-16
Tapestry of faiths: Introduction	17-19
Creation of Adam	21-23
Life in Eden	24-26
The Call of Abraham	28-30
The Binding of Isaac/Ishmael	31-33
Early Life and Mission of Moses	35-37
The Exodus and Ten Commandments	38-40
The Birth and Early Life of Jesus	42-44
Ministry and Teachings of Jesus	45-47
The Crucifixion and Resurrection/Ascension	48-50
Conclusion	51-52
Reflections on Shared Narratives and Divergent Paths	53-55
The Role of These Narratives in Contemporary Faith	56-58
Appendices	59-60
Comparative Tables	61-63
Glossary of Terms	64-66
Bibliography and Further Reading	67-69

TAPESTRY OF FAITHS:
THE TORAH, BIBLE, AND QURAN

INTRODUCTION TO "TAPESTRY OF FAITHS: THE TORAH, BIBLE, AND QURAN"

In a world often divided by differences, "Tapestry of Faiths: The Torah, Bible, and Quran" emerges as a beacon of understanding and harmony. This work is not just a book; it is a journey through the spiritual narratives that have shaped three of the world's major religions: Judaism, Christianity, and Islam.

At its core, this book aims to weave together the threads of these distinct yet interconnected faiths, offering readers a unique perspective on their shared histories and divergent paths. It delves into the narratives of key figures Adam, Abraham, Moses, and Jesus as seen through the lenses of the Torah, the Bible, and the Quran. By presenting these stories side by side, we illuminate the common ground they share and the differences that make each faith unique.

This comparative study is more than an academic pursuit; it is a call to mutual respect and understanding. In a time when religious differences are often highlighted, "Tapestry of Faiths" seeks to reveal the deeper connections that bind these traditions together. It invites readers of all backgrounds to explore the rich tapestry of stories and teachings that have guided millions of believers across centuries.

Tapestry of Faiths

As you turn these pages, you will embark on a journey through ancient times, experiencing the stories that have been told and retold, shaping the beliefs and cultures of countless people. This exploration is not just about understanding others; it is about understanding ourselves and the shared human quest for meaning and connection.

Welcome to "Tapestry of Faiths." Here, we do not seek to blend or blur the lines of distinct beliefs but to appreciate the beauty of each thread in the larger fabric of human spiritual history. Join us in this exploration of faith, history, and the common narratives that unite us all.

OVERVIEW OF THE PROJECT: "TAPESTRY OF FAITHS: THE TORAH, BIBLE, AND QURAN"

Project Vision and Purpose:

"Tapestry of Faiths" is an ambitious project designed to provide a comprehensive and comparative analysis of the shared and unique narratives found in Judaism, Christianity, and Islam. The primary aim is to foster interfaith understanding and respect by highlighting the commonalities and differences in the Torah, Bible, and Quran. This work seeks to bridge cultural and religious divides, offering a platform for dialogue and education.

Scope and Content:

The project focuses on four pivotal figures in these religious texts: Adam, Abraham, Moses, and Jesus. Each figure's story is examined across the three scriptures, providing insights into how each religion interprets and understands these shared prophets and historical figures.

1. **Adam:** Examining the creation story, the Garden of Eden, and the concept of disobedience and its consequences.

2. **Abraham**: Exploring the narratives of faith, covenant, and sacrifice, and how these are presented and understood differently.

3. **Moses**: Delving into the stories of liberation, law, and leadership, highlighting the role of Moses in each religion.

4. **Jesus**: Comparing the Christian portrayal of Jesus as the Son of God and Messiah with the Islamic view of him as a prophet, and noting his absence in Jewish scripture.

Methodology:

The project is grounded in scholarly research, utilizing a range of sources, including religious texts, theological commentaries, and academic studies. The approach is respectful, objective, and inclusive, ensuring that each faith's perspectives are presented accurately and fairly.

Audience:

"Tapestry of Faiths" is intended for a broad audience, including students of religion, interfaith groups, and anyone interested in understanding the similarities and differences among these three major world religions. It's also a valuable resource for those seeking to promote peace and mutual respect in multicultural and multireligious societies.

Outcome and Impact:

The ultimate goal is to create a resource that deepens understanding and appreciation of these rich religious traditions. By presenting these narratives side by side, the project aims to highlight the shared human experience and values that underlie all these faiths, fostering a sense of unity amidst diversity.

IMPORTANCE OF INTERFAITH UNDERSTANDING

Fostering Peace and Harmony:

In a world where religious misunderstandings often lead to conflict, interfaith understanding is crucial for creating a more peaceful and harmonious global society. By exploring and respecting the beliefs and practices of others, we can break down barriers of ignorance and mistrust, paving the way for greater cooperation and peace.

Enriching Personal Faith and Growth:

Engaging with different religious perspectives can deepen one's own faith and spiritual understanding. It encourages individuals to think critically about their beliefs, leading to a more profound and mature personal spirituality. This process of learning and reflection can be immensely enriching.

Promoting Social Cohesion and Respect:

In multicultural societies, interfaith understanding is key to social cohesion. It helps in building communities based on mutual respect and acceptance. This understanding can lead to stronger bonds between different community groups, fostering a sense of belonging and unity.

Educational Value:

Interfaith dialogue is a powerful educational tool. It broadens one's knowledge about the world and its diverse cultures and belief systems. Such education is vital in an increasingly interconnected world where cross-cultural interactions are common.

Challenging Extremism:

A lack of understanding about different faiths can fuel extremism. Interfaith dialogue counters this by debunking myths, stereotypes, and misconceptions that often feed into extremist ideologies. It promotes a more nuanced and balanced view of different religions.

Encouraging Empathy and Compassion:

Understanding the beliefs and values of others fosters empathy and compassion. It allows us to see the world from different perspectives, building a foundation for empathy and ethical behaviour towards those who may seem different from us.

Building a Foundation for Global Cooperation:

In a world facing global challenges like climate change, poverty, and health crises, interfaith understanding can lay the groundwork for unified responses.

By finding common ground in our shared human values, diverse religious communities can work together for the common good.

In summary, interfaith understanding is not a luxury but a necessity in our interconnected world. "Tapestry of Faiths: The Torah, Bible, and Quran" aims to be a significant step in this direction, opening doors to a deeper appreciation of the rich tapestry of human belief and the shared journey towards truth and understanding.

INTRODUCTION

In a world intricately woven with diverse cultures, beliefs, and traditions, the significance of understanding and appreciating the faiths of others cannot be overstated. "Tapestry of Faiths: The Torah, Bible, and Quran" embarks on an enlightening journey, delving into the heart of three of the world's major religions: Judaism, Christianity, and Islam. This exploration is not merely an academic endeavour; it is a quest for common ground, a search for the shared values and narratives that have shaped these faiths and, by extension, much of human history.

The importance of interfaith understanding in today's world is manifold. It is about fostering peace and harmony in a world often divided by differences. Understanding the religious beliefs of others helps bridge gaps, dispel ignorance, and break down the barriers of mistrust that have historically led to conflict. This understanding is a powerful tool for peace, promoting a dialogue based on mutual respect and shared values.

But the benefits of interfaith understanding extend beyond the realms of global peace and social cohesion. For individuals, engaging with the beliefs and traditions of other faiths can be a profound journey of personal growth and spiritual enrichment. It invites introspection and a deeper contemplation of one's own beliefs, leading to a more comprehensive and mature understanding of one's personal faith.

In societies that are increasingly diverse and multicultural, the importance of interfaith understanding becomes even more pronounced. It is a cornerstone for building communities where differences are not just tolerated but celebrated. Such understanding fosters a sense of belonging and unity, essential for social cohesion and harmony.

From an educational standpoint, interfaith dialogue broadens one's horizon, offering insights into the vast tapestry of global cultures and belief systems. In a world where cross cultural interactions are commonplace, such education is not just beneficial but necessary.

Moreover, at a time when extremism poses a significant threat, interfaith understanding plays a crucial role in countering radical ideologies. By offering balanced and nuanced views of different religions, it challenges the myths and stereotypes that often fuel extremism.

Perhaps most importantly, interfaith understanding cultivates empathy and compassion. It enables us to see the world through the lens of others, to understand their joys and sorrows, hopes and fears, thus fostering a global community built on empathy and ethical conduct.

In this light, "Tapestry of Faiths" is more than a book; it is a call to unity in diversity. It aims to illuminate the shared paths of Judaism, Christianity, and Islam, while respecting and celebrating their distinct journeys. This book invites readers on a voyage of discovery a journey toward deeper understanding, mutual respect, and shared human values. In a world where differences often lead to division, "Tapestry of Faiths" offers a harmonious chorus of diverse voices, united in their search for truth and understanding.

PART I: ADAM

CREATION OF ADAM

Comparative Analysis of the Creation Story

Introduction:

The story of Adam's creation is a narrative shared across the Torah, Bible, and Quran, each offering a unique perspective that reflects the broader theological and philosophical underpinnings of Judaism, Christianity, and Islam. This chapter explores these varying narratives to understand how the creation of Adam is portrayed and its significance in each of these Abrahamic religions.

Judaism The Torah's Account:

In the Torah, particularly in Genesis, Adam is depicted as the first human created by God. The narrative describes God forming Adam from the dust of the earth and breathing life into him. This act not only signifies the beginning of humanity but also highlights the intimate relationship between God and humankind. In Jewish thought, Adam's creation underscores the themes of human dignity and responsibility.

Christianity The Bible's Perspective:

The Christian account in Genesis mirrors the Jewish narrative, with additional emphasis on the theological implications of Adam's creation. In Christian theology, Adam is often seen as a figure representing humanity's fall and the need for salvation. The creation story in Christianity underscores the concept of original sin, with Adam's disobedience seen as the catalyst for humanity's fallen state and the eventual need for redemption through Jesus Christ.

Islam The Quranic Interpretation:

In Islam, the creation of Adam, as described in various surahs of the Quran, emphasizes his role as the first prophet and the first human. The Quranic account details how God created Adam and honoured him, teaching him the names of all things. In this narrative, Adam's creation is a testament to God's supremacy and the special place of humans in the divine order. Notably, the concept of original sin is absent in Islamic theology; instead, Adam's mistake and subsequent forgiveness are seen as a lesson in human fallibility and God's mercy.

Comparative Analysis:

While all three religions share the basic premise of Adam being the first human created by God, the interpretation and emphasis of the story vary. Judaism focuses on human dignity and responsibility, Christianity on the fall and redemption, and Islam on the nobility of Adam as a prophet and the mercy of God. These differences reflect each religion's core teachings and their understanding of the relationship between God and humanity.

Conclusion:

The creation of Adam is a foundational story in the Torah, Bible, and Quran, with profound implications in each tradition. By examining these narratives side by side, we gain insights into the shared heritage of these faiths and their distinct theological paths. This comparative analysis not only deepens our understanding of the story itself but also offers a window into the rich tapestry of beliefs and interpretations that define Judaism, Christianity, and Islam.

LIFE IN EDEN

The Garden, the Forbidden Fruit, and the Fall

Introduction:

The narrative of life in the Garden of Eden, encompassing the temptation, the eating of the forbidden fruit, and the subsequent fall, is a story of profound significance in the Torah, Bible, and Quran. This chapter delves into how each of these Abrahamic scriptures portrays this pivotal event in the early chapters of human history.

Judaism The Torah's Narrative:

In the Torah, the Garden of Eden is depicted as a divine creation, a place of perfection and innocence where Adam and Eve live in harmony with nature and under God's command. The Torah emphasizes the moral and ethical dimensions of the choice faced by Adam and Eve with the forbidden fruit. Their decision to eat from the Tree of Knowledge, against God's command, leads to their awareness of good and evil and their eventual expulsion from Eden. This act is often interpreted in Jewish thought as the moment when human beings gain moral consciousness and the freedom to choose.

Christianity The Bible's Account:

The Christian interpretation of the Eden narrative, found in Genesis, aligns closely with the Jewish account but is imbued with deeper theological implications. The act of disobedience by Adam and Eve is seen as the original sin that corrupts the inherent goodness of creation, introducing sin and death into the world. This event sets the stage for Christian doctrine on the need for salvation and redemption through Jesus Christ. The Eden story in Christianity underscores the frailty of human nature and the need for divine grace.

Islam The Quranic Perspective:

In the Quran, the story of Adam and Eve in the Garden carries themes of temptation, disobedience, and forgiveness. However, unlike the Torah and Bible, the Quran does not attribute the fall to sin or see it as a hereditary burden passed down to all humanity. Instead, it is viewed as a lapse on the part of Adam and Eve, for which they are forgiven upon repentance. The Quranic narrative emphasizes God's mercy and forgiveness, and the incident is seen as a lesson for humanity in accountability and the mercy of God.

Comparative Analysis:

While all three texts agree on the basic outline of the Eden narrative, their interpretations offer contrasting views on the nature and consequences of the fall. Judaism sees it as the beginning of moral consciousness, Christianity as the fall from grace necessitating redemption, and Islam as an instance of human fallibility and divine forgiveness. These differences reflect the distinct theological frameworks of each religion and their understanding of humanity's relationship with the divine.

Conclusion:

The story of the Garden of Eden, the forbidden fruit, and the fall is a cornerstone narrative in the Torah, Bible, and Quran, each offering a unique lens through which to view this early chapter of the human story. By exploring these narratives side by side, we gain a deeper appreciation of the shared themes and divergent teachings that these ancient texts offer, enhancing our understanding of Judaism, Christianity, and Islam. This comparative study not only enriches our knowledge of these religious traditions but also invites reflection on the broader questions of human nature, morality, and the divine.

PART II: ABRAHAM

THE CALL OF ABRAHAM

Journey, Covenant, and Trials in Different Scriptures

Introduction:

Abraham, a pivotal figure in Judaism, Christianity, and Islam, is renowned for his faith and obedience to God. This chapter examines the narrative of Abraham's call, his journey, the covenant with God, and his trials, as depicted in the Torah, Bible, and Quran. These stories not only highlight Abraham's significance in each faith but also illustrate the common heritage and distinct interpretations within these Abrahamic religions.

Judaism The Torah's Depiction:

In the Torah, Abraham (initially Abram) is called by God to leave his homeland and journey to Canaan. This act of leaving his home at God's command marks the beginning of the Jewish people. The covenant between God and Abraham is central, where God promises to make Abraham the father of a great nation. The binding of Isaac (Akedah) is a critical trial that tests Abraham's faith. In Jewish understanding, these narratives underscore themes of faith, obedience, and the beginnings of the Jewish nation.

Christianity The Bible's Interpretation:

The Christian Old Testament largely mirrors the Jewish account of Abraham. However, in the New Testament, Abraham's faith and righteousness are emphasized as precursors to Christian faith. The binding of Isaac is interpreted as a foreshadowing of God's sacrifice of Jesus Christ. Abraham's narrative in Christianity is often seen as an example of unwavering faith and trust in God's promises, serving as a model for Christians.

Islam The Quranic Perspective:

In Islam, Abraham (Ibrahim) is revered as a prophet and a model of pure monotheism. His rejection of idolatry and his unwavering commitment to God are central themes. The Quran includes stories of Abraham's trials, including his journey and his willingness to sacrifice his son (often interpreted as Ishmael rather than Isaac). These narratives emphasize Abraham's role as a model of submission to God's will and as a patriarch of the Islamic faith.

Comparative Analysis:

Abraham's story in the Torah, Bible, and Quran shares several elements, such as his call, journey, and the test of his faith. However, each scripture offers unique interpretations and emphasis.

Judaism views Abraham as the founding patriarch, Christianity as a precursor of faith and salvation, and Islam as a paragon of monotheism and submission to God. These interpretations reflect the theological and spiritual frameworks of each religion.

Conclusion:

The narrative of Abraham in the Torah, Bible, and Quran is a remarkable example of a shared story with varied meanings and implications in each tradition. Exploring these narratives side by side offers a window into the common roots and divergent paths of Judaism, Christianity, and Islam. Abraham's journey, covenant with God, and trials stand as a testament to his enduring legacy in these faiths, inviting believers and scholars alike to reflect on the depths of faith and the nature of divine human relationships.

THE BINDING OF ISAAC/ISHMAEL

Analysis of the Sacrifice Story Across Faiths

Introduction:

The story of the binding and near sacrifice of Isaac (in Judaism and Christianity) or Ishmael (in Islam) is one of the most powerful and pivotal narratives shared across the Abrahamic faiths. This chapter delves into the interpretations and theological significance of this story in the Torah, Bible, and Quran, exploring how each faith perceives this profound event.

Judaism The Torah's Portrayal:

In the Torah, the story known as the Akedah (the binding of Isaac) is a central narrative. God commands Abraham to sacrifice his son Isaac, a test of Abraham's faith and obedience. At the last moment, an angel intervenes, and a ram is offered in Isaac's place. This story is crucial in Jewish thought, symbolizing the depth of faith and the concept of not shirking from difficult trials. It is also interpreted as a condemnation of human sacrifice, a practice prevalent in some ancient cultures.

Christianity The Bible's Interpretation:

In the Christian Old Testament, this story aligns with the Jewish narrative. However, in Christian theology, it often takes on an additional layer of meaning, seen as a prefiguration of God sacrificing his own son, Jesus Christ. Isaac carrying the wood for the sacrifice is sometimes compared to Christ carrying the cross. Thus, the story in Christianity is seen through the lens of sacrifice, redemption, and divine providence.

Islam The Quranic Perspective:

The Quran does not explicitly name the son to be sacrificed; however, Islamic tradition often identifies him as Ishmael. In this narrative, Abraham's vision of sacrificing his son is a test of his and his son's submission to God's will. When they both show their willingness to comply, God intervenes and replaces the son with a ram. This story in Islam highlights themes of unwavering faith, submission (Islam), and the mercy of God. It's commemorated annually during the festival of Eid alAdha.

Comparative Analysis:

While the Torah and Bible focus on Isaac as the intended sacrifice, Islam usually considers Ishmael in this role. This difference is significant as it shapes the theological and historical perspectives of each religion. The common elements are the test of faith and the divine intervention to prevent the sacrifice, symbolizing God's mercy and the value of obedience and submission. Each faith draws different lessons from the narrative, reflecting their unique theological frameworks.

Conclusion:

The story of the binding of Isaac/Ishmael is a compelling example of how a shared narrative can hold different meanings and significance across religions. In Judaism, Christianity, and Islam, the story is a profound testament to faith, obedience, and divine benevolence. Analysing this story across the Torah, Bible, and Quran not only provides insights into the respective religious beliefs but also underscores the deep, interwoven history of these Abrahamic faiths. This chapter invites readers to contemplate the complex interplay of faith, ethics, and divine interaction in human affairs.

PART III: MOSES

EARLY LIFE AND MISSION OF MOSES

Birth, Encounter with God, and Return to Egypt

Introduction:

Moses is a central figure in Judaism, Christianity, and Islam, known for his leadership, prophecy, and the role he played in the liberation of the Israelites from Egyptian bondage. This chapter examines the narratives of Moses' early life, his encounter with God, and his return to Egypt, as portrayed in the Torah, Bible, and Quran. Each of these texts offers a unique perspective on his life and mission, reflecting the distinct theological contours of each faith.

Judaism The Torah's Depiction:

In the Torah, Moses' story begins with his miraculous preservation as an infant, floating down the Nile to escape a decree of death from the Pharaoh. Raised in the Egyptian royal court, Moses eventually flees to Midian after killing an Egyptian. His encounter with God occurs at the burning bush on Mount Horeb, where he receives the divine commission to return to Egypt and lead the Israelites to freedom. This narrative highlights Moses as a reluctant leader, chosen by God to deliver His people and bring them the Law.

Christianity The Bible's Account:

The Christian Old Testament recounts Moses' story similarly to the Jewish narrative. In the New Testament, however, Moses is often seen as a figure prefiguring Jesus, especially in his role as a lawgiver and mediator between God and people. Moses is revered as a prophet and a symbol of God's deliverance, and his life story is seen through the lens of salvation history.

Islam The Quranic Perspective:

In the Quran, Moses (Musa) is one of the most frequently mentioned prophets. His story includes his birth and upbringing, his flight to Midian, and his role as a prophet. The Quran provides additional details, such as his encounter with the two women at the well in Midian. His mission to confront Pharaoh and lead the Israelites out of Egypt is a significant part of his prophetic role. The Quran emphasizes Moses' steadfastness, his confrontations with Pharaoh, and his leadership qualities.

Comparative Analysis:

While the core elements of Moses' early life and mission are consistent across these texts, the focus and interpretation vary. Judaism emphasizes Moses as the lawgiver and leader of the Israelites, Christianity views him as a precursor to Christ and part of God's salvific plan, and Islam highlights his role as a steadfast prophet and a model of resilience. These interpretations reflect the unique theological themes of each religion.

Conclusion:

The narratives of Moses' early life and mission in the Torah, Bible, and Quran provide a fascinating insight into how this key figure is revered and understood differently in Judaism, Christianity, and Islam. His story is not just a historical or mythological account but is imbued with deep religious and ethical significance, shaping the beliefs and identities of these faiths.

By exploring these narratives, this chapter sheds light on the shared history and divergent paths of the Abrahamic religions and the enduring impact of Moses' legacy on their collective consciousness.

THE EXODUS AND TEN COMMANDMENTS

Liberation from Egypt and Revelation at Sinai

Introduction:

The Exodus and the revelation of the Ten Commandments are pivotal events in the history of the Abrahamic religions. These events mark the liberation of the Israelites from Egyptian slavery and the establishment of a covenant between God and His people through the giving of the Law. This chapter examines how these seminal events are recounted and interpreted in the Torah, Bible, and Quran.

Judaism The Torah's Narrative:

In the Torah, the Exodus is the dramatic escape of the Israelites from Egypt, led by Moses after God inflicts ten plagues upon Egypt. The crossing of the Red Sea and the journey to Mount Sinai are key events. At Sinai, Moses receives the Ten Commandments, a set of divine laws that form the cornerstone of Jewish law and ethics. This event is not just a historical liberation but also a spiritual awakening, signifying a special covenant between God and the Jewish people.

Christianity The Bible's Account:

The Christian Old Testament recounts the Exodus similarly to the Torah. The Ten Commandments are foundational in Christian ethics and morality. In the New Testament, these events are seen in the light of Christ's teachings. The Exodus is often interpreted as a symbol of spiritual freedom from sin, and the Commandments are viewed through the lens of Christ's emphasis on love and forgiveness.

Islam The Quranic Perspective:

In the Quran, the story of Moses leading the Israelites out of Egypt is also prominent. The narrative includes Moses' confrontations with Pharaoh and the miraculous crossing of the sea. While the Quran does not detail the Ten Commandments as in the Torah and Bible, it affirms the importance of the revelations given to Moses. These commandments are seen as part of a broader divine guidance that encompasses all Abrahamic prophets, including Muhammad.

Comparative Analysis:

All three religions view the Exodus as a significant act of divine intervention and liberation. Judaism focuses on the formation of a nation and a covenant, Christianity interprets it in the context of salvation and moral law, and Islam sees it as an example of God's power and guidance.

The Ten Commandments in Judaism and Christianity are central to their ethical teachings, while in Islam, the emphasis is on the broader concept of divine guidance given to Moses and other prophets.

Conclusion:

The narratives of the Exodus and the Ten Commandments play a crucial role in shaping the religious and moral landscape of Judaism, Christianity, and Islam. These events are not only historical milestones but also profound revelations that continue to influence the ethical and spiritual lives of believers.

By exploring these narratives, this chapter highlights the shared heritage of these faiths and their distinct theological interpretations, offering a deeper understanding of their foundational stories and principles.

PART IV: JESUS

THE BIRTH AND EARLY LIFE OF JESUS

Nativity Stories and Early Years

Introduction:

The story of Jesus' birth and early life holds significant importance in Christianity and Islam, while it is absent in Jewish tradition. This chapter explores the narratives of Jesus' nativity and early years as presented in the Bible and the Quran, highlighting the similarities and differences in these accounts and their implications in both religions.

Christianity The Bible's Account:

In the New Testament of the Bible, particularly in the Gospels of Matthew and Luke, the nativity story is a cornerstone of Christian faith. It describes the miraculous conception of Jesus by the Virgin Mary, his birth in Bethlehem, the angelic announcement to shepherds, the visit of the Magi, and the subsequent flight to Egypt to escape King Herod's decree. These events are celebrated in Christianity as the incarnation of God in Jesus Christ, symbolizing God's closeness to humanity and the beginning of the fulfilment of prophetic promises.

Islam The Quranic Perspective:

In the Quran, Jesus (Isa) is also born to the Virgin Mary (Maryam) in a miraculous event. The Quran emphasizes the miraculous nature of Jesus' birth without a father and Mary's piety and faith. The story includes Mary's isolation, the pain of childbirth under a palm tree, and Jesus speaking as a baby to defend his mother's honour. In Islam, Jesus is revered as a prophet and his birth is viewed as a sign of God's power and a testament to the miraculous.

Comparative Analysis:

While both Christianity and Islam acknowledge the miraculous birth of Jesus to the Virgin Mary, the significance and interpretation of these events differ markedly. In Christianity, Jesus' birth is the incarnation of God and central to the faith's understanding of salvation and redemption. In Islam, while Jesus is highly honoured as a prophet, his birth, though miraculous, does not signify divine incarnation but rather is a demonstration of God's ability to accomplish the extraordinary.

Conclusion:

The narratives of Jesus' birth and early life in Christianity and Islam provide a fascinating insight into how a shared figure is viewed differently in these two religions. These stories not only reflect the theological and doctrinal distinctions between Christianity and Islam but also highlight the respect and reverence both religions have for Jesus. This chapter not only enriches our understanding of the nativity narratives but also fosters a deeper appreciation for the shared yet distinct heritage of these faiths.

MINISTRY AND TEACHINGS OF JESUS

Miracles, Parables, and Teachings

Introduction:

Jesus' ministry, characterized by his teachings, parables, and miracles, is a period of profound religious and historical significance, particularly in Christianity and Islam. This chapter examines the depiction of Jesus' ministry in the New Testament of the Bible and the Quran, focusing on the themes, teachings, and miraculous acts attributed to him, and how they are interpreted differently in these two faiths.

Christianity The Bible's Account:

In the New Testament, Jesus' ministry is a central narrative. His teachings, which include the Sermon on the Mount, parables like the Good Samaritan, and directives such as the Great Commission, form the foundation of Christian doctrine. The miracles of Jesus, such as healing the sick, raising the dead, and feeding the multitudes, are seen as signs of his divinity and the inauguration of the Kingdom of God. His teachings emphasize love, forgiveness, and the reversal of social norms, calling for a deep, personal commitment to God and a transformation of the heart.

Islam The Quranic Perspective:

In Islam, Jesus (Isa) is revered as a prophet and messenger. The Quran acknowledges his miraculous birth and attributes several miracles to him, including speaking as an infant, healing the blind, and raising the dead, all by God's permission. The teachings of Jesus in the Quran emphasize monotheism, righteousness, and submission to God's will. However, the Quran refutes the divinity of Jesus and considers his miracles and teachings as signs of his prophethood.

Comparative Analysis:

While both Christianity and Islam recognize the miraculous aspects of Jesus' life and his role as a teacher, their interpretations diverge significantly. In Christianity, Jesus' ministry is the fulfilment of prophecy and central to the faith's understanding of salvation, with his miracles seen as evidence of his divine nature. In contrast, Islam views Jesus' miracles as a testament to God's power and Jesus' role as a prophet, not as divine. The teachings of Jesus in Islam align with Islamic theology, emphasizing strict monotheism and moral righteousness.

Conclusion:

The ministry and teachings of Jesus, as presented in the Christian and Islamic scriptures, offer a window into the theological and doctrinal heart of these two religions. This chapter not only illuminates the similarities and differences in how Jesus' life and work are understood but also reflects the broader religious and cultural contexts in which these narratives developed. By exploring these accounts, readers gain a deeper appreciation of the profound impact of Jesus' ministry across different faith traditions and its enduring influence in the religious and ethical discourse of humanity.

THE CRUCIFIXION AND RESURRECTION/ASCENSION

The Christian Perspective and Islamic Interpretation

Introduction:

The narratives of Jesus' crucifixion, resurrection, and ascension are pivotal in Christian theology and are also addressed in Islamic texts, albeit with significant differences. This chapter explores these events as depicted in the Christian Bible and the Islamic Quran, highlighting the profound theological divergences that these accounts represent in each faith.

Christianity The Bible's Account:

In Christianity, the crucifixion of Jesus is central to the faith. It is seen as the fulfilment of God's plan for the salvation of humanity, with Jesus sacrificing himself for the sins of the world. This act of atonement is followed by his resurrection, which Christians believe is a confirmation of Jesus' divinity and the promise of eternal life for believers. The ascension of Jesus into heaven is viewed as the final act of his earthly ministry, signifying his return to divine glory and his ongoing presence in the lives of believers.

Islam The Quranic Perspective:

The Islamic view, as presented in the Quran, differs significantly. Islam denies the crucifixion and death of Jesus. Instead, it is believed that Jesus was not crucified but was raised up by God unto Himself. The Quran states that it appeared to the people that Jesus was crucified, but this was not the case. In Islam, Jesus is regarded as a prophet whose message was in line with the messages of other prophets: to worship the one true God. His ascension is seen as a sign of his esteemed status in the eyes of God.

Comparative Analysis:

The Christian and Islamic narratives of the end of Jesus' earthly life represent a fundamental theological divergence between the two religions. For Christianity, the crucifixion and resurrection are the cornerstone of faith, symbolizing Jesus' victory over sin and death. In Islam, the emphasis is on the exaltation of Jesus as a prophet, with a rejection of the crucifixion and resurrection narratives as they are understood in Christian doctrine. This distinction highlights the differing perspectives on Jesus' nature and mission in Christianity and Islam.

Conclusion:

The stories of the crucifixion, resurrection, and ascension of Jesus are more than historical events in religious narratives; they are reflections of deep theological beliefs that shape the faith and practice of billions of believers. This chapter not only sheds light on these crucial episodes in Christian and Islamic theology but also invites readers to reflect on the profound implications of how Jesus' life and legacy are interpreted in these two major world religions. The exploration of these differing narratives provides valuable insights into the core tenets that define Christianity and Islam, enhancing our understanding of these faiths and their view of one of the most significant figures in religious history.

CONCLUSION

Reflections on Shared Narratives and Divergent Paths:

"Tapestry of Faiths: The Torah, Bible, and Quran" has journeyed through the shared narratives of Judaism, Christianity, and Islam, exploring their common roots and the distinct paths they have taken. This exploration reveals a tapestry rich in shared heritage, yet unique in theological interpretation and cultural expression. The stories of Adam, Abraham, Moses, and Jesus highlight a profound interconnectedness at the heart of these Abrahamic faiths, pointing to a common ancestry of belief and tradition.

Yet, as our journey demonstrates, these shared narratives also diverge significantly, creating distinct identities for each faith. These divergences are not merely historical or academic; they reflect deep theological and philosophical differences that have shaped cultures, societies, and individual lives. Understanding these differences is crucial in appreciating the unique perspectives each religion brings to the dialogue of faith.

The Role of These Narratives in Contemporary Faith:

In today's world, where religious beliefs often intersect, clash, and coexist in complex ways, the role of these narratives extends beyond historical or theological interest.

They are living stories that continue to shape the identities, ethics, and worldviews of billions of people around the globe. For practitioners of these faiths, these stories are not just ancient texts but are integral to their understanding of the divine, the world, and their place within it. They offer guidance, inspiration, and a sense of belonging to a tradition that transcends time and space. For scholars and interfaith activists, these narratives provide a rich ground for dialogue, understanding, and building bridges of mutual respect and cooperation.

In a world often divided by misunderstanding and intolerance, a deeper engagement with these stories can be a source of unity and peace. By recognizing the shared heritage and respecting the divergent paths, adherents of these faiths can find common ground in their quest for meaning, purpose, and the divine.

Conclusion:

"Tapestry of Faiths: The Torah, Bible, and Quran" invites readers to view these ancient narratives not just as relics of the past but as living dialogues between faiths. The stories of these texts continue to speak to us, offering wisdom, challenging our perceptions, and calling us to a deeper understanding of our neighbours and ourselves. In a world yearning for peace and understanding, these narratives can be a beacon, guiding us towards a future where different faiths can coexist in harmony and mutual respect, celebrating both their shared roots and their unique branches.

REFLECTIONS ON SHARED NARRATIVES AND DIVERGENT PATHS

Shared Heritage and Common Ground:

The exploration of the Torah, Bible, and Quran in "Tapestry of Faiths" highlights a significant shared heritage among Judaism, Christianity, and Islam. These Abrahamic religions, rooted in a common ancestral faith, share numerous narratives, figures, and ethical teachings. This shared lineage underscores a profound interconnectedness, suggesting an inherent unity in the spiritual quests of these faiths.

Divergent Interpretations and Paths:

Despite this shared heritage, the paths of Judaism, Christianity, and Islam diverge significantly in their theological interpretations, ritual practices, and religious laws. These divergences are not just historical footnotes; they are living streams of religious thought and practice that have shaped the identities of communities and individuals over millennia. Each religion has developed its unique understanding of the divine, the role of humanity, and the path to spiritual fulfilment.

The Role of Context and History:

The differences in these religious narratives can often be attributed to the historical and cultural contexts in which they evolved. As these faiths encountered various political, social, and intellectual environments, their teachings adapted, leading to new interpretations and practices. Understanding these contexts is crucial for appreciating the reasons behind the divergent paths of these religions.

Contemporary Relevance:

In a modern world marked by religious pluralism and global interaction, the importance of understanding these shared narratives and divergent paths cannot be overstated. This awareness fosters mutual respect and opens avenues for dialogue and cooperation. Recognizing our shared heritage can be a powerful antidote to the divisiveness and conflict that often arise from religious misunderstandings.

Interfaith Dialogue and Understanding:

The comparative study of the Torah, Bible, and Quran is an exercise in interfaith dialogue, promoting a deeper understanding of and respect for each tradition. It highlights the importance of empathy and open-mindedness in approaching religious texts and traditions other than one's own.

By engaging with the similarities and differences in these sacred texts, believers and non-believers alike can gain insights into the rich tapestry of human spiritual expression.

Conclusion:

The shared narratives and divergent paths of Judaism, Christianity, and Islam, as explored in "Tapestry of Faiths," serve as a reminder of our common human quest for understanding the divine. They invite us to celebrate both our shared roots and our unique branches, encouraging us to build bridges of understanding in a world that deeply needs empathy and mutual respect.

This journey through the scriptures of these faiths is not just a historical or academic exploration; it is a journey towards a deeper understanding of the human spirit and its longing for connection, meaning, and transcendence.

REFLECTIONS ON SHARED NARRATIVES AND DIVERGENT PATHS

Shared Heritage and Common Ground:

The exploration of the Torah, Bible, and Quran in "Tapestry of Faiths" highlights a significant shared heritage among Judaism, Christianity, and Islam. These Abrahamic religions, rooted in a common ancestral faith, share numerous narratives, figures, and ethical teachings. This shared lineage underscores a profound interconnectedness, suggesting an inherent unity in the spiritual quests of these faiths.

Divergent Interpretations and Paths:

Despite this shared heritage, the paths of Judaism, Christianity, and Islam diverge significantly in their theological interpretations, ritual practices, and religious laws. These divergences are not just historical footnotes; they are living streams of religious thought and practice that have shaped the identities of communities and individuals over millennia. Each religion has developed its unique understanding of the divine, the role of humanity, and the path to spiritual fulfilment.

The Role of Context and History:

The differences in these religious narratives can often be attributed to the historical and cultural contexts in which they evolved. As these faiths encountered various political, social, and intellectual environments, their teachings adapted, leading to new interpretations and practices. Understanding these contexts is crucial for appreciating the reasons behind the divergent paths of these religions.

Contemporary Relevance:

In a modern world marked by religious pluralism and global interaction, the importance of understanding these shared narratives and divergent paths cannot be overstated. This awareness fosters mutual respect and opens avenues for dialogue and cooperation. Recognizing our shared heritage can be a powerful antidote to the divisiveness and conflict that often arise from religious misunderstandings.

Interfaith Dialogue and Understanding:

The comparative study of the Torah, Bible, and Quran is an exercise in interfaith dialogue, promoting a deeper understanding of and respect for each tradition. It highlights the importance of empathy and open-mindedness in approaching religious texts and traditions other than one's own.

By engaging with the similarities and differences in these sacred texts, believers and non-believers alike can gain insights into the rich tapestry of human spiritual expression.

Conclusion:

The shared narratives and divergent paths of Judaism, Christianity, and Islam, as explored in "Tapestry of Faiths," serve as a reminder of our common human quest for understanding the divine. They invite us to celebrate both our shared roots and our unique branches, encouraging us to build bridges of understanding in a world that deeply needs empathy and mutual respect.

This journey through the scriptures of these faiths is not just a historical or academic exploration; it is a journey towards a deeper understanding of the human spirit and its longing for connection, meaning, and transcendence.

APPENDICES

Appendix A: Comparative Tables

1. **Table of Prophets:** A comparative table listing significant prophets and figures as they appear in the Torah, Bible, and Quran.
2. **Timeline of Events:** A chronological table comparing key events and narratives in Judaism, Christianity, and Islam.
3. **Theological Concepts:** A table comparing important theological concepts like the nature of God, sin, salvation, and the afterlife across the three faiths.

Appendix B: Glossary of Terms

A comprehensive glossary providing definitions and explanations of terms, names, and concepts unique to Judaism, Christianity, and Islam. This section will aid readers unfamiliar with specific religious terminology.

Appendix C: Annotated Bibliography and Further Reading

A curated list of recommended books, articles, and resources for further exploration of the topics covered in the book. This bibliography will include both religious texts and scholarly works.

Appendix D: Maps and Historical Illustrations

1. Maps illustrating the geographical context of key biblical and Quranic stories.
2. Historical illustrations and artworks depicting scenes from the Torah, Bible, and Quran.

Appendix E: Commentary and Exegesis

A selection of commentary and exegesis from Jewish, Christian, and Islamic scholars, providing deeper insights into specific passages or stories from the Torah, Bible, and Quran.

Appendix F: Interfaith Dialogue Resources

Resources and guidelines for engaging in interfaith dialogue, including contact information for interfaith organizations and initiatives.

Appendix G: Reflections and Meditations

1. A collection of reflections and meditations inspired by the narratives and teachings from the Torah, Bible, and Quran, intended to provide spiritual insight and contemplation for readers from diverse faith backgrounds.

COMPARATIVE TABLES

Table 1: Comparative Table of Prophets

Prophet / Figure	Judaism (Torah)	Christianity (Bible)	Islam (Quran)
Adam	First man, lived in Eden	First man, original sin	First prophet, no original sin
Noah	Survivor of the Flood, covenant with God	Survivor of the Flood, symbol of salvation	Prophet, preacher of God's message
Abraham	Founder of Jewish nation, covenant with God	Father of faith, covenant with God	Prophet, model of monotheism
Moses	Liberator of Israelites, lawgiver	Prefiguration of Jesus, lawgiver	Prophet, leader against Pharaoh
David	King of Israel, psalmist	Ancestor of Jesus, king	Prophet, king, given Psalms
Solomon	Wise king, built the Temple	Wisdom and wealth, son of David	Prophet, known for wisdom and ruling
Elijah	Prophet, miracles, opposed idolatry	Prophet, herald of the Messiah	Prophet, known for piety and miracles
Isaiah	Prophet, messianic prophecies	Prophet, foretold Jesus' birth	Mentioned as a prophet

Prophet / Figure	Judaism (Torah)	Christianity (Bible)	Islam (Quran)
Jesus	Not a figure in Jewish scripture	Son of God, saviour, crucified and resurrected	Prophet, not crucified, ascended to heaven

Table 2: Timeline of Key Events

Event	Judaism (Torah)	Christianity (Bible)	Islam (Quran)
Creation	Genesis account	Genesis account	Creation of the world and humanity
The Flood	Noah's Ark	Noah's Ark	Noah and the great flood
Exodus	Liberation from Egypt, Ten Commandments	Same as Torah, symbol of salvation	Moses leads Israelites, confronts Pharaoh
Birth of Jesus	Not applicable	Virgin birth in Bethlehem	Miraculous birth to Mary (Maryam)
Crucifixion of Jesus	Not applicable	Crucified, resurrected	Not crucified, raised to heaven

Table 3: Theological Concepts

Concept	Judaism (Torah)	Christianity (Bible)	Islam (Quran)
Nature of God	One, indivisible	Trinity: Father, Son, Holy Spirit	One, indivisible, no partners
Sin	Moral failing, breaking commandments	Original sin, moral failing	Disobedience to God, no original sin
Salvation	Following commandments, repentance	Faith in Jesus, grace	Righteous deeds, faith, God's mercy
Afterlife	Concept of Sheol, later belief in resurrection	Heaven and hell, resurrection	Heaven (Paradise) and hell, resurrection

These comparative tables offer a succinct overview of key figures, events, and theological concepts as they are presented in the Torah, Bible, and Quran, highlighting both the shared heritage and distinct interpretations within Judaism, Christianity, and Islam.

GLOSSARY OF TERMS

This glossary provides definitions and explanations for key terms and concepts found in "Tapestry of Faiths: The Torah, Bible, and Quran", enhancing understanding of the shared and unique aspects of Judaism, Christianity, and Islam.

Akedah: A term used in Judaism referring to the binding of Isaac by Abraham as a test of faith. It's a central story in the Torah.

Allah: The Arabic word for God, used in Islam.

Apostle: In Christianity, one of the early followers of Jesus, specifically chosen to spread his teachings.

Caliph: A title in Islam, meaning 'successor', used for the leader of the Muslim community after the death of Muhammad.

Covenant: A key concept in both Judaism and Christianity, referring to the agreement between God and His people.

Eid al:Adha: An Islamic festival commemorating the willingness of Abraham to sacrifice his son in obedience to God.

Gospel: In Christianity, the accounts of the life and teachings of Jesus, especially the books of Matthew, Mark, Luke, and John in the New Testament.

Hadith: In Islam, a collection of traditions containing sayings of the prophet Muhammad which, with accounts of his daily practice, constitute the major source of guidance for Muslims apart from the Quran.

Halakha: The collective body of Jewish religious laws derived from the written and Oral Torah.

Imam: In Islam, the person who leads prayers in a mosque; also a title for various Muslim leaders, especially in Shia Islam.

Messiah : In Judaism, the promised deliverer of the Jewish nation prophesied in the Hebrew Bible. In Christianity, Jesus is regarded as the Messiah.

Prophet: A person regarded as an inspired teacher or proclaimer of the will of God. In Islam, Muhammad is considered the last prophet.

Quran: The holy book of Islam, believed to be the word of God as revealed to Muhammad.

Resurrection: In Christianity, the belief that Jesus rose from the dead on the third day after his crucifixion.

Sharia: Islamic law based on the Quran and Hadith, covering all aspects of Muslim life.

Talmud: The central text of Rabbinic Judaism and the primary source of Jewish religious law (Halakha) and Jewish theology.

Trinity: In Christian doctrine, the unity of Father, Son, and Holy Spirit as three persons in one Godhead.

Zakat: One of the Five Pillars of Islam, involving giving a fixed portion of one's wealth to charity.

This glossary provides a foundational understanding of terms that are essential for exploring the rich tapestry of beliefs, practices, and theological concepts in Judaism, Christianity, and Islam.

BIBLIOGRAPHY AND FURTHER READING

The following bibliography and list of resources offer further exploration into the topics covered in "Tapestry of Faiths: The Torah, Bible, and Quran." These materials include religious texts, scholarly works, and additional readings that provide deeper insights into Judaism, Christianity, and Islam.

Religious Texts:

1. **The Torah** - The central reference of the Jewish religion.
2. **The Bible** - Including both the Old Testament (shared with Judaism) and the New Testament, central to Christian faith.
3. **The Quran** - The holy book of Islam, believed to be the word of God as revealed to the Prophet Muhammad.

Scholarly Works and Commentaries:

4. **"A History of God:** The 4,000-Year Quest of Judaism, Christianity, and Islam" by Karen Armstrong - A comprehensive exploration of how the concept of God has evolved in the three religions.
5. **"Judaism, Christianity, and Islam:** The Classical Texts and Their Interpretation" by F.E. Peters - A detailed study of the key religious texts and their interpretations in these faiths.

6. **"The Bible, the Quran, and Science" by Maurice Bucaille** - An analysis of the scriptures in the light of modern scientific knowledge.
7. **"The Abrahamic Religions:** A Very Short Introduction" by Charles L. Cohen - A concise overview of Judaism, Christianity, and Islam.

Contemporary Discussions:

8. **"The Faith Club:** A Muslim, A Christian, A Jew-- Three Women Search for Understanding" by Ranya Idliby, Suzanne Oliver, and Priscilla Warner - A personal narrative of interfaith dialogue.
9. **"God Is Not One:** The Eight Rival Religions That Run the World" by Stephen Prothero - A book that discusses how different world religions, including Judaism, Christianity, and Islam, are distinct in their understanding of God and salvation.

Interfaith and Cultural Studies:

10. **"The Children of Abraham:** Judaism, Christianity, Islam" by F.E. Peters - An examination of the shared heritage and distinct features of the three faiths.
11. **"Interfaith Dialogue:** A Guide for Muslims" by Mohammad Shomali and William Skudlarek - Insights into engaging in meaningful interfaith dialogue.

Online Resources and Journals:

12. **Journal of Inter**-Religious Studies
13. **Interfaith.org** - A website dedicated to exploring the similarities and differences between religions.
14. **The Pluralism Project at Harvard University** - An online resource providing information on religious diversity in the United States, including studies on Abrahamic faiths.

~~~~~~~~~~~~~~~~~END~~~~~~~~~~~~~~~~~

www.ingramcontent.com/pod-product-compliance
Lightning Source LLC
Chambersburg PA
CBHW021123080526
44587CB00010B/618